IN

As you may have noticed, this is a pretty short book. That's intentional, and it's done for a very specific purpose. The ideas laid out here aren't things you should spend a lot of time reading about; they're things you should spend a lot of time doing.

This book isn't arranged in any particular order, so feel free to just jump to any page and see if that particular date idea would be a good fit for you, your date, and your current situation.

These dates are all designed to work for you regardless of your gender, and regardless of your financial background (all of these dates are inexpensive, and many are completely free).

These dates have been selected so that they will work great in a first date situation, where you don't know your partner very well, but these dates will also work for couples who have known each other for years.

So needless to say, all of the ideas you're about to discover are very flexible.

Most of the date ideas in this book are fairly simple, and that's done on purpose as well. The more complicated a date is, the more it will detract from the main point of the date: helping two people get to know each other. So don't let the simplicity of these date ideas make you think that they're inferior to more elaborate dates; these ideas have been gathered from the world's top dating experts, and they work. Give them the respect they deserve, and you (and your date) will be well rewarded.

TIPS FOR SUCCESSFUL DATING

Every type of date is different, and creates a different kind of vibe, but there are some guidelines that should be followed no matter what kind of date you're on.

Be Flexible

When planning a date, allow for some wiggle room just in case problems crop up. If you have to be someplace at 7:00, don't plan on arriving at 6:55. There may be traffic issues on the way there, your date may show up late, etc. Don't let little hitches like this spoil the evening.

Use the Element of Surprise

Most people like surprises, and if you handle it right, it can be a lot of fun to whisk your date away to some kind of mystery location. It almost doesn't matter where you're going: the whole way there your date will be trying to figure it out, and that's the fun part.

The thing to watch out for when doing this is to make sure that when your date actually figures out what the activity will be for the evening, it's not a let-down.

You don't have to build the date up; in fact, it's probably best if you tell them that the date itself is nothing special, you just want to surprise them. The sense of mystery will still be a lot of fun for them, and they won't be let down when they find out that you aren't taking them on a helicopter ride over the Grand Canyon.

Likewise, try and make the date at least a little bit interesting or funny. It will seem weird to take your date somewhere as a surprise, only for them to find out that the "big surprise" is something fairly ordinary like a coffee shop. The date doesn't have to be fancy, just a little out of the ordinary.

Leave an escape plan

Regardless of whether this is your first date or your 500th, things may not go well and it may be best to call it a night early. If it's your first date, you may not like them and they may not like you. If you're married, your spouse may start to not feel well, or one of you may get an emergency phone call.

So when you're planning your date, don't trap yourselves some-where it would be difficult or awkward to leave from. You can do this by either planning short dates, or dates that you can make short because you're at a location where you're free to stay as long or as short a time as you want and can easily leave at a moment's notice.

Don't spend a fortune

Even if you're rich, spending a ton of money on a date isn't a good idea. Dates are supposed to be about 2 people making a connection, not about showing off.

The best experiences are usually not the most expensive. For ex-ample, which sounds like a better date: a walk down a moonlit beach, or dinner at an expensive restaurant? The walk on the beach is at least as good as the restaurant (better, in my opinion), and it happens to be free.

If you paid a lot for a date and it doesn't go well, you'll be sorry you wasted your money. If your date only likes you because you're feeding them caviar, you don't want to be dating them in the first place.

So don't let other people call you cheap or pressure you into spending a lot of money. Most of the dates in this book will run you less than $10-$15, which is more than enough to have an amazing experi-ence.

Don't do dinner and a movie

This one is so common that I have to mention it specifically. I'll spell it out very clearly: dinner and a movie is boring and cliché. Don't do it. You can do some similar things to this, which we'll cover in a second, but for now, just get it into your head that just because this is popular (and, in fact, precisely because it's popular) that doesn't make it a good idea.

So without further ado…let's get on with the dates!

DATE IDEAS

Horrible Movie

I'm going to mention this one right off the bat, because it's the exception to the rule when it comes to doing "dinner and a movie" (which is normally lame).

(Incidentally, I actually don't recommend you do dinner with this one, because that makes for a long evening).

Just go see a movie, but when you're picking the movie out, DON'T try and think of one that your date will like, and DON'T try and think of one that's entertaining. Try and pick a movie that is really weird.

The exact kind of weirdness is up to you, but what I recommend for this situation is that you deliberately find a movie that is horrible, just so you and your date can spend the evening making fun of it and laughing at how bad it is.

Normally going to a movie involves sitting in the dark side-by-side and not interacting, which is pretty much the exact opposite of what dating is intended for. The great thing about this date is that it's interactive and really memorable. It will also loosen you and your date up, and create a fun atmosphere for the evening.

Conan the Barbarian
Total Recall

Shopping and Cooking

Putting these two mundane activities together creates a really cool, intimate experience. Basically what you're going to be doing is bringing your date along with you to the grocery store to buy ingredients with you, and then bringing them home where the two of you will be turning those ingredient into a meal.

First of all, just to get it out of the way: you don't have to be a good cook. All you have to do is find a recipe online or in a cookbook somewhere that seems pretty easy to make, and try it out. If you've never made the recipe before, your date will actually be kind of excited that they get to do something with you that you've never done before.

One thing that's very important about this is that you aren't just inviting your date straight over to your place and cooking the meal for them while they sit around. They are helping you shop, and helping you cook. You can send them to go hunt for certain ingredients while you're in the grocery store, have them chop ingredients for you while you're handling another aspect of the food preparation, etc. It's an interactive experience, where the two of you are working on a project together, and that will make the two of you "bond" way more than if your date were just to sit around watching you cook.

All day, every day

Toy Store

This one is simple: just bring your date to a toy store and goof around.

You can play with the various toys, for starters (building things with Legos, throwing Nerf balls around, etc).

If you have a digital camera, you can take pictures of your date posing with an enormous teddy bear or wearing a silly costume.

You can even give your date a budget (something ridiculously small, like 2 dollars), and tell them that they can have anything in the store as long as it's under that amount. Having them run around trying to find something within their tiny budget is good fun.

This is a cool date because it will allow you and your date to revert back to childhood, and recapture that innocence and fun together. Probably something your date doesn't get a chance to do very often.

Beaches

There are two kinds of beaches you can go to depending on where you live: an ocean beach, or a lake beach. Either way, you probably have a beach of some kind near where you live. Obviously the ocean is better, but if you don't live on the coast, work with what you've got.

There are two ways you can do the beach thing. The first involves going at night, the second involves going during the day.

Being on a moonlit beach is obviously really romantic, which can be good or bad depending on what you're going for. A moonlit beach has become kind of a romantic cliché (despite the fact that no one seems to actually do it anymore), so if you're worried about the whole thing seeming cheesy, go during the day.

Going to a beach during the day can be a lot of fun if you pick the right time and the right beach. Otherwise, you may be surrounded by a beach-full of screaming kids and their cranky parents.

Either way, there are several types of beach dates you can do. You can go to just splash around in the water and sunbathe, you can go rollerblading along the water, or you can have a picnic.

You'll have to use your best judgment on what type of activity to do, but all of the above options (and more) are strong possibilities, just because the beach is such a cool place to do pretty much anything.

Boating Tour

If you live near a river, ocean, or other large body of water, chances are that you'll be able to find a boating tour or boat cruise of some kind. These generally last anywhere from one to three hours. Depending on what type of cruise/tour you find, you will get varying degrees of autonomy: on smaller boats there will often be a tour guide who will point out landmarks and such, while on larger boats you will mostly be left to wander the boat and take in the sights on your own. This latter type of cruise is probably better, because it gives you and your date more "alone time" to talk and get to know each other.

Lobster Tour

Kayaking

Go Karts

Going to a Go Kart track can be a great way to get you and your date's adrenaline going without actually doing anything that's actually hard or intimidating. It can also create a really fun, competitive vibe between the two of you that will give a fun, playful context to the two of you spending time together.

York Beach

Homemade Ice Cream

This may sound like it would be difficult, but making homemade ice cream is actually pretty easy. The ingredients are simple: cream, vanilla, sugar, salt, and ice. And, although your date has probably cooked with someone before, they probably haven't made ice cream on a date before, so this is pretty much guaranteed to be a unique experience for them.

A nice touch is to find out what kind of ice cream your date likes and make that. This is really simple: just whip up a batch of vanilla ice cream, and then add whatever your date likes: cookie dough, chopped up candy bar pieces, etc.

Sample day

Find a grocery store that has a "sample day" (a day where they give out tons of free samples to customers, usually a weekend), and take your date there to stroll around and try all the free stuff.

This has to be done in a tongue-in-cheek way, so that your date knows you aren't just a lame cheapskate. But there's lots of room for playful banter here, and if you're in one of those big warehouse stores, it can be fun to stroll around, check out the merchandise, and act like a couple on a shopping trip. It's a fun role-play, and a quirky way of getting a free meal.

Thrift Store Makeover

Take your date to a thrift store, and together pick out the most gaudy, ridiculous outfits you can find. Make all the weird clothing and accessory combinations you can find, until you and your date both look like homeless clowns. Buy all the stuff (each item will only cost a maximum of a few bucks, and many pieces will cost a dollar or less).

Get dressed up in your new outfits, and go stroll around a public place together where there are a lot of "normal" people around, like a park or mall. Act normal, and just go about your business as if nothing is out of the ordinary at all. You and your date can enjoy turning heads together, and be sure to bring a camera!

Car Wash

Here's a cool, low-key date for nice weather: bring your date over and have them help you wash and wax your car. Do this the old-fashioned way, with buckets and your garden hose, rather than just going to a car wash. You can also go to your date's place and wash and wax their car, if you're looking to do something nice for them.

On paper this may seem like a chore, but in real life it's actually very relaxed and fun...unless you decide to start using the hose on them, in which case things might get a little crazy.

Lot of times

Pet store

This one is just adorable: take your date to a pet store. You can interact and play with a large number of the animals, and the ones you can't interact with (like the fish) are still fun to watch and marvel at.

A nice thing about this is that all of the affection your date feels (while petting puppy dogs, holding bunny rabbits, etc.) will get associated to you since the two of you are sharing this experience. Just be careful not to let any of the animals charm you into taking them home with you.

People Watching

Basically, you're just going to go to some public place where there are lots of people (a public park, the mall, etc.) and people-watch with your date. The two of you can make a game out of sizing people up and trying to figure out what kind of person they are and where they're going, and just generally "playing detective" by observing the people around you.

This is nice because it creates the vibe of you and your date being in a little world together from which the two of you look out and examine the rest of the world. It can be very intimate if done properly.

Day in Day Out
From Paris to Lowell

Playground

This one may seem utterly ridiculous, but give it a try and you'll see how fun it is. All you're going to do is take your date to a playground and play. Simple, right? You can take turns pushing each other on the swings, go down the slides, hang from the monkey bars, and just act like kids.

You should probably pick a time when the playground isn't going to be full of kids, just so that you and your date don't feel too self-conscious surrounded by kids and parents staring at you (and to make sure you don't accidentally squish some kid by coming down the slide too fast).

Everyone loves reconnecting with their childhood, but nobody really ever does anything childish. This is a great way to bring out your date's (not to mention your own) childish, playful side.

Saturday morning cartoons

Here's another awesome childish thing to do: invite your date over to watch Saturday morning cartoons, just like when you were kids.

Don't half-ass it though: get a bunch of sugary cereal, wear your pajamas, and curl up on the couch together covered in blankets. It makes for a great morning.

✓

Winery tour

Most places have a winery at least somewhat nearby, even if the area is not known for wine-making at all (for example, as many as 48 out of the 50 U.S. states have wineries). So chances are that there's a winery somewhere near you, probably not more than an hour away.

Chances are also good that you can do a wine-tasting for free (or very inexpensively), because most wineries know that the more people try their wine, the more people will end up buying it. So a winery tour can be a very inexpensive and beautiful date if you're willing to take a bit of a drive.

Done that

Surprise gift shopping

You and your date each get a small amount of money (preferably something very small, like $5, to make this more of a challenge), and turn yourselves loose in a large multi-department store (such as Target, Walmart, etc.). The goal: the two of you split up, and each of you are assigned the task of buying a surprise gift for the other person.

The limited amount of money you each have to work with requires you to be creative, which is what makes this date fun. Not to mention the fact that in order to keep your gifts a surprise, you'll have to sneak around the store like spies, keeping an eye out for your date to make sure they don't accidentally see what you're getting them.

Each of you is to check out separately, hide your gift in a bag, and meet at the store entrance. Then it's up to you where you want to go in order to exchange gifts.

Fake Millionaire

This one requires a little bit of creativity in order to make it work. Basically, you're going do something with your date that you would normally only be able to do if you were rich, but in order to avoid the high price tag, you're going to do the "free or cheap version" of that activity.

What does this mean? Here are some examples:

You can go to an obscenely fancy restaurant and just order a cup of coffee or a dessert (you'll be able to enjoy the exact same amazing service and opulent surroundings as the people paying for full meals, and you can people-watch all the rich folks).

You can test drive a ridiculously expensive sports car that you could never afford to buy (test drives are free, after all).

You can go to open houses for high-end homes and spend an afternoon strolling through fabulous mansions.

There are endless possibilities for this type of date, so brainstorm your own list of ideas and then go date like a millionaire.

✓

Ben + Becky, Virginia Beach

Newspaper Birthday

This one is short and simple. First, you'll need to find out your date's birthday. After you have this information, go to a public library and use the newspaper archives (I believe they're called "microfiche"; ask your librarian), and try to find the archived historical newspaper for the exact year, month, and day that your date was born.

Once you've done a trial run and found the newspaper, it will be easy for you to find it again when you bring your date there to look through the newspaper with you (don't read the newspaper on your first run-through, otherwise it will spoil the surprise) to see what was happening in the news on the day that they were born. You can also show your date what the newspaper said on your birthday.

Volunteer

Basically, instead of doing something for yourselves, you and your date are going to do something for other people, by volunteering for a charity. A great way to do this is by volunteering to serve a meal at a soup kitchen/homeless shelter, but there are lots of other options as well. You can go around and collect food for a food bank, do some yard work or house work for an elderly person in your neighborhood, etc.

This may be a little heavy for a first date, so if you have any doubts save it for later, but it's also really unique and very socially responsible, so give it some consideration. Even if the date doesn't go well, it will have been time well spent.

The zoo

A lot of people associate a trip to the zoo with children, but zoos are really fun for adults as well. Admission is usually cheap (and sometimes even completely free, depending on what part of the country you live in), and it's fascinating to stroll around together and look at the incredible variety of exotic wildlife.

Feeding the Birds

This one is really simple: buy a loaf of cheap bread, go to a lake, and feed the ducks and geese. Doesn't get much simpler or cheaper than that, but the lake is a beautiful setting and it's fun to watch the birds running around gobbling up the bread while you and your date talk.

Stargazing

Looking up at the stars is classically romantic, but unfortunately it's a physical impossibility for most people, because the "light pollution" from cities and towns makes the stars invisible from the locations where most of us actually live.

Fortunately, it's still pretty easy to go stargazing, you just have to be willing to drive. If you and your date have the time, drive to an uninhabited area out in the middle of nowhere that won't suffer from light pollution (state and national parks work well for this). The drive itself will be fun and scenic for you and your date, and of course being out in the wilderness under the stars is amazing. Just make sure that you find a spot with a lot of open space above you (preferably on a hill) so you can enjoy the entire panorama of the sky.

If you were a city-kid growing up, and you've never been out in the middle of the wilderness at night, you will be absolutely astounded by how beautiful the night sky is when you're seeing it in its true form, without all the light pollution from human habitation getting in the way.

Origami

Get a few different books of origami patterns from the library, and then either buy some sheets of nice origami paper (which are always very inexpensive, even if the paper is really nice) or just use regular white copy paper that you probably have already laying around.

You'll invite your date over, and each of you will pick a different origami pattern that you like out of the books that you got. If you have 2-4 origami books, you will have literally several hundred different origami figures to choose from, some of which can be quite elaborate and beautiful.

Once you each have picked out a figure that you like, the two of you will sit side by side at your table and follow the instructions, giving each other help as needed (and possibly having to start over several times). You don't need any origami experience for this at all, since you just have to follow the instructions in the book.

When you and your date have both finished, you can decide to either keep your figures as a memento from your date, or you can exchange your figures as gifts for each other.

Playing in the rain

This date is very flexible: all you're going to do is take an outdoor activity that you would normally do in nice weather, and instead do it in the middle of a rainstorm.

You can do pretty much any outdoor activity you want for this; anything from mini-golf to playing catch/Frisbee, or even just going for a walk in the park. The activity itself doesn't have to be anything special at all, because the whole point is that you and your date are going to be frolicking around splashing each other and jumping in mud puddles.

This is an extremely fun date. The only problem is that you have to wait for it to rain. Rather than trying to coordinate this date for a day when the forecast is rainy, you might want to just plan an outdoor date for a certain day that you would enjoy doing anyway, and then hope that it rains!

Boating

Pretty much every decent-sized lake and river you can find will have some kind of boat or canoe rental service set up when the weather is nice. There may be one or more different types of boat to choose from: canoes, kayaks, paddle boats, etc.

Depending on what kind of "vessel" you rent, this will usually be very cheap, and you can spend a leisurely afternoon paddling around on the open water, just chatting and enjoying the day.

Kayaking
Meredith + Steve

Moonlight swim

This really isn't that different from swimming during they day, but it's a lot more romantic. Pick a place to swim (this can be anything; a pool at a park or a hotel, even a lake) and go swimming by moonlight.

A really nice touch for this is to light some candles on the side of the pool, and even better is if you can rig up the candles on some kind of flotation device so that they will float next to you and your date in the water.

Driving range

Taking your date to a driving range can be fun regardless of whether or not either of you actually plays golf. You can rent both golf balls and golf clubs relatively cheaply at most places, so you don't have to own your own equipment, and even though golf is a difficult sport to excel at, you don't have to be athletic to try it out, like you do with most sports.

If you happen to play golf, this can be a great opportunity to give you date an informal "lesson" which can be fun. But it's almost better if both of you are terrible at golf, so that the two of you can enjoy watching each other screw around.

Flea Market

Taking your date to browse around in a flea market can be a lot of fun, and by definition it's an activity that is both unusual and extremely cheap.

Check the internet and your local newspapers to find local flea markets, swap meets, etc. Some of these are held outdoors, and some are held inside (in places like malls). Generally they take place once a week, usually on the weekend. You can also check out crafts fairs, which are generally a little more artistic and a little less eccentric (although not by much).

Since most of the enjoyment from this activity just comes from ogling all the weird merchandise, you don't necessarily have to spend a single penny on this date.

Out of place

Go to a bar or club that caters to a demographic you and your date don't belong to. For example, if you and your date are kind of the clean-cut preppy type, go to a goth bar. If you and your date are tattoo-and-piercing-covered punk rockers who like to dress in all-black, go to the bar at a golf course/country club.

You and your date should both have somewhat thick skin and a good sense of humor for this date, because you'll probably get some dirty looks, but being the only two-of-a-kind in the room is a great bonding experience. Even if something crazy happens and you get kicked out, it just makes the date that much more memorable.

Award-Winning Birthday Movie

This is similar to the newspaper idea mentioned previously, but requires less leg-work, so it's a better option for you if you're feeling lazy. All you have to do is look up what movie won the Academy Award for Best Picture of the Year for the year that your date was born, then rent that movie and watch it with your date. It's a fascinating look at what popular culture was like on your date's first day in the world.

Reliving Your School Years

If you ever attended a college or university (and have already grad-uated), take your date to your campus and give them a tour, showing them all of the significant spots like your dorm, your favorite spot to study, the buildings where you had your favorite and least-favorite class-es, the bar where you got caught trying to use a fake ID, etc.

You can probably even do this if you're currently in college, as long as your date doesn't attend the same school (otherwise they obviously wouldn't need a tour).

Roadside attractions

No matter where you live, you definitely live within easy driving distance of some kind of roadside attraction. It doesn't matter whether it's something kind of quirky, like the world's biggest ball of yarn, or something more ordinary, like the highest or lowest elevation point in your state. Taking your date to this kind of location makes for a fun mini road trip. Do some research and you'll probably find dozens of odd little roadside attractions near where you live.

Fireplace S'mores

    The name pretty much says it all: if you have a fireplace, invite your date over to make s'mores with you in your living room. Simple, fun, inexpensive, and doesn't require you to organize an entire camping trip.

    If you don't have a fireplace, most public parks have fire pits that you can use, all you have to do is bring your own firewood.

Planetarium

This is heavily dependent on where you live, but if your city has a planetarium, it makes for an interesting (albeit somewhat nerdy) date location. These places usually have "shows", which are either guided tours of the stars or laser light shows, as well as miscellaneous exhibits in the surrounding buildings.

If your date is kind of a science geek, this will be the perfect place to take them.

Go for a Hike

There's nothing particularly unique or exciting about this activity when you look at it on paper, but for most of us who grew up in a city or suburb, going on hikes is actually a pretty rare thing.

There are probably all kinds of hiking trials near where you live, either in the countryside outside of your city, or even within some of your area's larger parks.

Spending an afternoon out in nature is an increasingly uncommon thing. But getting out and soaking up all of that fresh air and sunshine will put you and your date in a great mood, and leave you both feeling revitalized at the end of your date.

Give blood

This isn't exactly a "romantic" activity in the normal sense of the word, but there's something kind of cool about you and your date sitting side by side, each with a needle in your arm, donating something valuable to help a good cause.

Yes, it's kind of weird, but in a good way: it's definitely different, and it will leave your date feeling good about doing a good deed.

Build a Snowman

This one is really fun and self-explanatory: you and your date just go somewhere nice and build a snowman together. You can either keep it simple, or bring some "props" with you; clothes, material for making facial features, etc.

This can be done in a public park, but it's probably better to do it in your yard (or your date's). The only drawback to this date is that there has to be enough good, wet snow on the ground in order to do it, so it's not an option for certain seasons and certain parts of the country.

Disc Golf

Frequently referred to by the improper name of "Frisbee Golf" ("Frisbee" is a brand name, not the name of the object), disc golf is challenging but also very easy to get into; all you need is a disc to throw.

If you don't know what disc golf is, feel free to look it up online. Since it just involves throwing a disc around, it's a very leisurely game that is easy to get into if you aren't very athletic. Many large parks have disc golf areas, and they're completely free to use, so if you're got your own disc this date is completely free.

Off-Roading

This date involves renting an ATV ("all-terrain vehicle", kind of like a 4-wheel drive Go Kart) and using it to explore beautiful, rugged outdoor areas that would be otherwise inaccessible.

A lot of ATV rental places offer "tours", in which a guide will take a group of people out on a guided tour. These tours are best avoided: you're tied to the rest of the group during the tour, so you can't stop when you want, you can't go where you want, and you won't have any alone time with your date.

Off-roading is an exciting activity that allows you to do something active and fun, and get off the beaten path with your date.

Unusual Sport

If you want to take your date to a sporting event, consider taking them to something a little bit more unique than the standard baseball/football/basketball game.

Some examples of unusual sports include polo, rugby, lacrosse, even curling. Going to see one of these sporting events has all the same benefits as going to see a popular sport, but it's much more unique and memorable, and since the games are less popular, they're often cheaper, which is a nice bonus.

Rollen Dench

Rock Climbing

Rock climbing makes for a really fun, challenging date.

If you associate rock climbing with going out and climbing a mountain, that's not what we're talking about here: instead, what you're going to do is find an indoor rock climbing gym and take your date there.

Indoor rock climbing is much more accessible, safe, and inexpensive than climbing outdoors, and most cities have a climbing gym. If there aren't any in your area, you can check for rock climbing "walls", which are smaller and often located inside of stores that cater to rock climbing and mountaineering.

Rock climbing is great because it will get you and your date's adrenaline pumping, and you can take a class together to learn how to "belay" each other (hold your partner up via the rope while they're climbing). Belaying is extremely easy, but it requires you to put your personal safety in someone else's hands, which will create a real bond of trust between you and your date.

City Lights

This is a simple date; it just involves finding a secluded spot with an amazing view of the city at night and having a picnic while you lay back, watch the city lights, and talk.

The particular spot you pick doesn't have to be special, it just has to have a great view of the city. This may take some exploring, but chances are that you've already noticed a spot with a great view while traveling around your area. It can be a bridge or the top of a building, but the traditional location would be on top of a hill somewhere over-looking the city.

A nice touch is to bring some candles so that the two of you can see your picnic by candlelight.

Fly a Kite

This one is pretty simple, but there are a few guidelines you should follow to make this run as smoothly as possible. Basically, if you want to fly a kite, there are certain locations which are ideal (lots of open space, no obstructions to the wind) and weather conditions (right amount of wind and so on).

In order to make sure that you have all the factors correct, go talk to someone at a local kite shop to see if they can recommend a good place and time for kite flying (and sell you a good, inexpensive kite).

Other than that, this date is very simple, relaxed, and fun.

Share music

For this date, you and your date will each put 10 of your favorite songs of all time on an mp3 player, go somewhere nice to hang out, and then take turns listening to each other's songs.

For the most part you'll actually just be talking like on a normal date, but the whole time you and your date will be getting to know each other's tastes in music through your respective musical selections. This is a great way to get to know your date, and provides a fun context for an otherwise ordinary date.

Be an Expert

Most people are talented at something, or at least passionate about a particular subject. This date gives you the chance to share that passion.

Basically what you're going to do is teach your date how to do a favorite activity. You can teach them anything: chess, tennis, piano, yoga, car repair, photography – pretty much anything.

This allows you to "show off" something that you're good at in front of your date, teaches them something, and creates a lot of interaction and byplay between the two of you.

Picking Fruit

There are certain farms all over the country that allow people to come and pick their own fruit for a nominal fee. These farms are great places to go on dates.

Generally the way this works is that you either buy a container which you are free to fill up, or you bring your own container and pay by the pound. You and your date will have fun walking through beautiful orchards and farmland picking the fruit, and when you're done you'll have more fruit than either of you can eat, which you can give to friends and family.

Dog Walking

If you happen to own a dog, bringing your date along with you while you take the animal out for a stroll makes for a great date.

Obviously you won't do this for a quick walk around the block, but when you take your dog out to play catch or take them to a dog park, invite your date along. Dogs are obviously extremely playful and affectionate, so your date will love having the opportunity to play with you and your animal companion, and it gives the two of you something to do while you get to know each other.

Local College Events

Colleges and universities are always having free events for their students, and the vast majority of these events are actually open to the public.

To find these events simply go to a nearby college's website and look in their "event calendar" and you will see options for free events like outdoor movies, interesting lectures, open mic/karaoke night, concerts and more.

Glow in the Dark Catch

Get yourself a glow-in-the-dark ball or Frisbee, go to a football field, park, or beach, and play catch. Wear glow in the dark necklaces to see where the other person is, and you can even wear a glowing band around your "catching wrist" to see where each other's hands are. Play catch for a while and then watch the stars.

Random road trip

Pick a random small town near where you live that you've never been to before, and go there with your date on a mission of exploration. Try and pick a town that's really small: if you grew up in an urban or suburban environment, it's a real head trip to spend the day in a town where the population is smaller than your high school.

You and your date can explore the town a little bit, have lunch at a local diner, and just generally have yourselves a relaxing, sight-seeing afternoon. You might want to look at the town's website the night before to see if there are any appealing activities in the area, and once you're there be sure to stop by the visitor center for more ideas.

Photo Albums

Spend an evening showing your date your old photo albums and high school yearbooks. Find a cozy place to sit with lots of room to spread out and got through the old photos chronologically, and if your date is willing, have them do the same thing for you with their old albums as well.

While looking at the photos, you can even have your date try to guess what's happening, where the picture was taken, what time of year it was, etc. (before you fill them in).

The pictures in these books will be lots of fun to share, and this is a guaranteed night of laughing together. You and your date will learn a lot about each other as you share the stories and experiences behind each picture.

Conclusion

There you have it! You've just finished learning 51 different unique, inexpensive, and fun dating ideas.

Now is where the most important part comes in: actually going on these dates! Don't just let this book sit on your shelf and never get used because you're unwilling to try something new. Some of these dates will probably put you a little outside your comfort zone, but that's exactly what makes them fun.

So get out there, experiment with these ideas, and try these dates out in the real world. You (and whoever you decide to take with you) will be happy you did.

Made in the USA
Lexington, KY
16 February 2012